OXFORD
First Book of
Animals

OXFORD
First Book of
Animals

Barbara Taylor

OXFORD
UNIVERSITY PRESS

OXFORD
UNIVERSITY PRESS

Great Clarendon Street, Oxford OX2 6DP

Oxford University Press is a department of the University of Oxford.
It furthers the University's objective of excellence in research, scholarship,
and education by publishing worldwide in

Oxford New York

Auckland Bangkok Buenos Aires Cape Town Chennai
Dar es Salaam Delhi Hong Kong Istanbul Karachi Kolkata
Kuala Lumpur Madrid Melbourne Mexico City Mumbai Nairobi
São Paulo Shanghai Taipei Tokyo Toronto

Oxford is a registered trade mark of Oxford University Press
in the UK and in certain other countries

British Library Cataloguing in Publication Data available

ISBN 0–19–910985-0 Paperback

1 3 5 7 9 10 8 6 4 2

Printed in China

Contents

What is an Animal?   6

On the Move   8

Eyes, Ears and Noses   10

Hungry Animals   12

Hunting and Hiding   14

Eggs, Babies and Growing Up   16

Living Together   18

Minibeasts   20

Animals with Shells   22

Fishes   24

Reptiles and Amphibians   26

Birds   28

Mammals   30

Grasslands   32

Forests   34

Deserts   36

Cold Places   38

Oceans and Shores   40

Animals in Danger   42

Animal Detective Quiz   44

Index   46

What is an Animal?

From tiny insects and sponges, to huge bears and eagles, animals come in all shapes and sizes. There are probably more than 15 million different kinds of animal living today. They are organised into groups. By far the biggest group is animals without backbones. These are called invertebrates. Animals with backbones are called vertebrates. Most animals have several things in common: they eat other living things, use their senses to detect their food, and move around to catch it.

▼ This colourful male mandrill is a kind of monkey. Monkeys are mammals, and so are we!

Animals without backbones

Invertebrates do not have bones, but they may have a hard skin or shell for support and protection, either inside or outside their body. Most invertebrates, such as jellyfish, live in the sea. Some, such as insects, live on land. A few invertebrates, such as sea anemones, look more like plants than animals.

▼ Arthropods, such as insects, crabs and spiders, all have jointed legs and a body in several segments, covered by a hard outer case. More than 75 per cent of all animals are arthropods.

▲ Worms are animals that have a long, soft body without any legs. There are three main kinds: flatworms, round worms and segmented worms, such as this earthworm.

▼ Molluscs have a soft body, usually with a hard shell around it. Snails are molluscs, so are octopuses and oysters.

Animals with backbones

A typical vertebrate usually has a skeleton inside its body, with muscles attached to the bones. It also has powerful senses and a relatively large brain. The largest and brainiest animals are vertebrates, such as dolphins, elephants and people. There are five main types of vertebrate: fish, amphibians, reptiles, birds and mammals.

▶ Mammals are the only animals with fur or hair. Even this elephant has some hair. Baby mammals drink milk from their mother's body. There are about 4,000 different kinds of mammal.

▶ Birds are the only animals with feathers. They have wings instead of arms, and most birds can fly.

▶ Reptiles live mainly on land and have a scaly skin. Tortoises, lizards, snakes and crocodiles are all reptiles.

◀ Amphibians live partly in the water and partly on land. They have a smooth skin, four legs and lungs for breathing air. Newts, frogs and toads are all amphibians.

▼ Fishes live in water. They have scaly bodies, fins, and gills to help them breathe underwater.

What do animals do?

Animals spend their time finding food, keeping warm or cool, avoiding danger, finding a mate and producing young. To help them survive, animals use their senses as well as their ability to move. This makes them different from plants, which make their own food and cannot move around.

▲ Waxwings eat berries and insects, so they eat both plants and animals. Some animals eat only plants, others eat only animals.

▶ Most animals, such as this jaguar, can move their whole body and travel from place to place.

▶ A squirrel's large eyes and ears help it to watch and listen for danger.

7

On the Move

Walk, run, hop, jump, crawl, slither, slide, swim, fly and glide . . . animals move in all sorts of ways. They move to find food, escape danger, keep warm or cool, to find a mate and care for their young. The way an animal moves depends on its size, its shape and its surroundings. But all moving animals push backwards to drive themselves forwards. They also keep changing shape as they move, because their muscles pull parts of their bodies into different positions.

Legs on land

You move around on two legs, but most land animals have four, six or eight legs. Millipedes have more than a hundred legs! Legs have to be carefully controlled by muscles and nerves, so animals don't trip over their own feet.

The cheetah is the fastest animal on land. It can run as fast as a car. When the cheetah sprints, all four feet come off the ground.

8

Wings and flying

Only birds, bats and insects are able to fly, by flapping their wings. A bird's wings are its front arms, with feathers over the top. A bat's wings are its hands, with skin stretched over long finger bones. An insect's wings are made of extra bits of its hard body-covering.

◄ A bird has powerful muscles to beat its wings up and down. This pushes air downwards and backwards to keep the bird up in the air.

Fishy swimmers

Most fish swim by bending their whole body, or just their tail, from side to side. This pushes against the water to drive them along. The fins on the side of a fish's body help it to steer, balance and brake.

► Flying fish can glide above the waves for several hundred metres to escape enemies.

◄ The sailfish is the fastest fish in the sea, zooming along at up to 100 kilometres per hour.

Look Closer

Some animals have special tails, toes or other parts of the body to help them move more easily.

► The spider monkey has a strong tail that grips branches like an extra hand.

◄ The flying opossum spreads out flaps of skin along the sides of its body. These work like a furry parachute so it falls down slowly and can glide from tree to tree.

► The sharp, non-slip hoofs of mountain goats help them to cling to the rocks on steep mountain slopes.

Eyes, Ears and Noses

Animals use their senses of sight, hearing, smell, taste and touch to find out what is going on in the world around them. This helps them to find food, keep away from danger and move around safely. Animals also use their senses to help them communicate with each other.

▲ Wasps have two big compound eyes, made up of lots of little eyes joined together, and three simple eyes.

Sight

Most animals have eyes to see with. Eyes pick up light as it bounces off things. They may sense movement or build up a picture of an animal's surroundings. Some animals, such as birds, butterflies and humans, can see in colour. But most mammals, such as cats, dogs and horses, see only in black and white.

▼ Night-time animals, like this bushbaby, often have huge eyes to help them see in the dark.

Hearing

Some mammals, such as bushbabies, have big ears to catch sounds as they move through the air. Mammals are the only animals with ear-flaps on the outside of the head. A few animals don't have ears on their heads. Did you know that crickets have ears on their legs?

A shrew's eyes are very small and its eyesight is poor. To move around and find food, a shrew uses its keen senses of smell, hearing and touch. Long whiskers on its pointed nose are sensitive to touch.

Smell

We can detect about 10,000 different smells, but a dog's sense of smell is about a million times better than ours. Many animals have a nose for smelling things, but insects smell with their antennae and snakes smell with their tongue!

Ring-tailed lemurs spread scent from their wrists and bottoms onto branches to tell other lemurs to keep out of their area. Males even smear scent onto their tails and wave them at their rivals, to drive them away.

Look Closer

Snakes use their senses of smell, taste and touch more than their sight and hearing. Some snakes, such as boas and pythons, can also sense the heat given off by their prey. Special heat holes on their faces pick up this heat.

▶ A snake flicks out its forked tongue to taste and smell the air.

Hungry Animals

Animals need food to stay alive. They cannot make their own food, so they have to eat plants or other animals. Animals such as bears and foxes eat almost anything. A few animals, such as koalas, eat only one kind of plant. An animal usually has to break up food into small pieces to swallow it. Some animals, such as crocodiles, swallow their food whole.

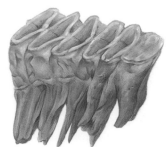

The sharp ridges on an elephant's tooth help to cut up its food.

Plant eaters

Animals such as cows, horses and caterpillars eat plants. Plants are tough to chew and do not contain much goodness. Plant eaters have to spend a lot of time eating to survive.

Meat eaters

Animals such as dogs and snakes eat meat. They hunt other animals and often have to work hard to get a meal. But meat is full of goodness, and many meat-eaters can survive for days or weeks without eating.

Wolves hunt together in packs, so they can kill animals much larger than themselves, such as deer, bison and mountain sheep.

Activity

Make a bird-feeding bell to give birds a safe feeding place out of reach of cats.

You will need: an empty yoghurt pot, string, scissors, a mixing bowl and spoon, melted lard (about 100 grams), bird food - such as birdseed, nuts (not salted), raisins, breadcrumbs, oats and cooked rice.

1 Make a small hole in the bottom of the pot. Thread a long piece of string through the hole and tie a large knot in the end to keep it in place.

2 Ask an adult to melt the lard in a saucepan while you mix up the bird food in the bowl. Pour the melted lard over it.

3 Spoon the mixture into the yoghurt pot and leave it in a cool place until it goes hard.

4 Hang the bell on a tree branch or the side of a bird table, and watch the birds feed.

Ways of eating

Animals usually take food into their bodies through a mouth opening. Some animals, such as flies and mosquitoes, suck up liquid food through a sort of 'straw'. Other animals use teeth, jaws or beaks to break up their food before they swallow it.

▶ A spider's mouth is too small for solid food. It uses its jaws and other mouthparts to mash up food into a kind of soup.

▽ A curlew pushes its long bill into the mud to find juicy worms.

▶ A flamingo's bill is like a sieve. It filters out tiny bits of food from the water.

◁ A giant anteater pushes out its long, sticky tongue 150 times a minute to lick up ants and termites.

▶ An eagle tears up meat with its sharp, hooked bill.

13

Hunting and Hiding

Most hunting animals are bigger and stronger than their prey. To find and catch a meal, they need good senses and speedy movement. Some hunters are patient and cunning. They build traps, lie in wait or sneak up on their prey without making a sound. To stop being caught, prey animals may hide away, or defend themselves with sharp claws, spines, horrible smells or cunning tricks.

Weapons

Special weapons help animal hunters to attack and kill their prey. These might be long, sharp claws, pointed teeth or fangs. Spiders and some snakes have a poisonous bite to kill their prey quickly, before they themselves get hurt.

▲ Swooping down from the sky, a bird of prey such as this osprey catches and holds its prey with razor-sharp talons. Ospreys have spiny scales on their toes to grip slippery fish.

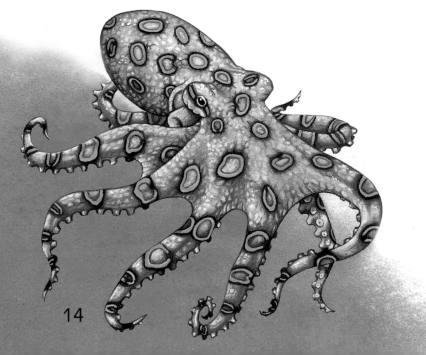

◄ The tiny blue-ringed octopus paralyses crabs with its poisonous saliva, then moves closer to gobble up its meal. Its bright colours warn that it is very poisonous. One octopus has enough poison to paralyse 10 adult men.

14

Fighting back

To hide from hunters, prey animals are often camouflaged. Others stay out in the open, but can run very fast to escape from their enemies. If they have to defend themselves, some prey animals use weapons such as sharp claws and spiky coats; others may rely on body armour for protection.

▲ This grass snake is pretending to be dead. Hunters prefer to catch and eat living animals, so they leave the grass snake alone.

▲ A porcupine rattles its quills and stamps it feet to make enemies go away. If they don't, it sticks its sharp quills into their skin.

▲ A skunk's black and white stripes warn enemies to keep away. If it is attacked, the skunk sprays the enemy with a very smelly liquid.

▲ Porcupine fish puff themselves up with water or air, making their spines stick out. This makes them too big for most hunters to swallow.

Look Closer

Coral reef fishes escape from their enemies in many different ways. Some, such as the wobbegong shark, are well camouflaged to blend in with the background. Others, such as the boxfish, have coats of armour for protection.

These clown fish hide in the stinging tentacles of sea anemones. They cover themselves in a layer of slime so they don't get stung. The clown fish's bright colours may warn enemies of the anemone's dangerous tentacles, and help to keep both animals safe.

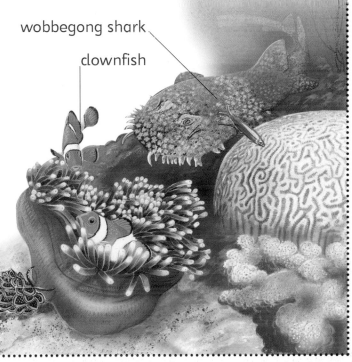

wobbegong shark

clownfish

Eggs, Babies and Growing Up

Baby animals either hatch out of eggs or are born from their mother's body. Some baby animals, such as dogs and horses, look like their parents. Others, such as butterflies and frogs, look very different at first then change the shape of their bodies so they look like their parents.

▼ A baby elephant stays really close to its mother, but all the elephants in a family group help to look after it. They protect it from enemies such as snakes and lions, and shade it from the hot sun.

A baby owl cuts its way out of the egg (a). The new chick is blind and almost naked (b), but it soon develops feathers (c). At 19 days old, it takes its first wobbly steps (d). At two months it can fly (e).

a

b

c

d

e

Mother scorpions sometimes carry their young on their backs until they can look after themselves. Some scorpions have up to 90 babies at a time.

Look Closer

A butterfly goes through four stages in its life. It starts out as an egg, which hatches into a caterpillar. The caterpillar eats and grows, and changes into a pupa. Inside the pupa, the body of the caterpillar is turned into a sort of soup and is re-built into an adult butterfly with wings. This big change is called metamorphosis.

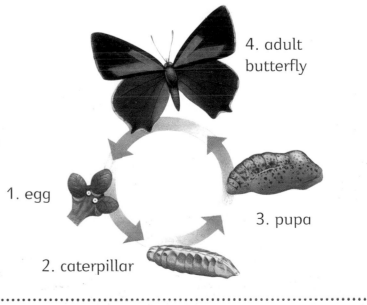

4. adult butterfly

1. egg

3. pupa

2. caterpillar

Living Together

Some insects and mammals live in groups with others of their own kind. This is very useful because they can help each other to find food, watch out for danger and bring up their young. In mammal groups, older animals may teach younger ones how to survive. Different kinds of animals may also team up if they can help each other in some way.

Insect cities

Ants, termites and many kinds of bee and wasp each live together in giant family groups that build special homes. Thousands, or even millions, of insects live in these insect cities. Only one female, called the queen, lays eggs. The other insects share out the work of looking after the nest, eggs and young.

▶ Termite towers can be taller than a person and take up to 50 years to build. They are made of rock-hard soil that it is impossible for most enemies to dig through. Inside the towers, it is warm, moist and completely dark.

▼ The queen and king termite live in the royal chamber. The queen lays thousands of eggs each day.

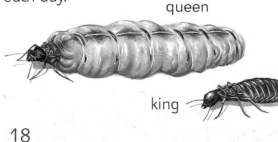

queen

king

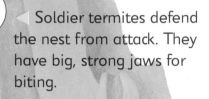

▼ Termites with wings, called alates, hatch out once a year. They fly away to build new termite cities.

◀ Soldier termites defend the nest from attack. They have big, strong jaws for biting.

▲ Most of the termites are workers who collect food, look after the young and repair the nest.

The termites eat little mushrooms, which they grow in gardens inside their tower.

food stores

nurseries for the eggs and young termites

royal chamber

▽ You can tell how a chimp is feeling from the expression on its face. Here are three different ones to look out for:

▲ A mother chimp spends six years or more looking after her young. Young chimps learn how to behave and take care of themselves by watching the adults in their family group, and by playing games with their brothers, sisters and friends.

▲ angry face: lips shut tight

▲ play face: bottom teeth showing

▷ excited or frightened face: mouth open, all the teeth showing

Animal partners

Different animals sometimes live together because they can give each other food or protection. On coral reefs, small cleaner fish and shrimps feed on food scraps, dead scales and anything growing on the skin of much bigger fish. The cleaners have a meal and the bigger fish stay healthy.

▷ This sweetlips fish holds its mouth open, so a cleaner wrasse can pick its teeth clean.

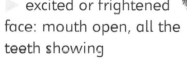

19

Minibeasts

Minibeasts are small animals such as wriggly worms, buzzing bees, slimy snails and scary spiders. Three out of every four animals in the world are minibeasts. The main thing they have in common is that they do not have a backbone to support their bodies. Many minibeasts, such as lobsters and jellyfish, live in the sea, but others - especially insects - are very common on land.

Hunt the minibeast

Go on a minibeast hunt in your garden or local park and see how many different kinds you can find. Many will be hidden away, so look carefully under stones, logs or leaves, in the soil, on walls or fences, in compost heaps or on tree bark.

▶ Insects, such as butterflies, bees and beetles, are the most common animals in the world. There are at least five million kinds! They all have six legs and three parts to their body. Most have wings and feelers, called antennae.

Snails have a shell but most slugs do not. They both belong to the same group of animals.

Millipedes and centipedes have lots of rings, or segments, and lots of legs too! Millipedes can have as many as 350 legs. Most centipedes have 30 legs. Millipedes are usually plant-eaters, but centipedes are hunters of insects.

Worms have a long, thin body with no legs. An earthworm's body has lots of rings, called segments. It eats its way through the soil to look for dead plant material to eat.

▶ Most crustaceans, such as lobsters, shrimps and this coconut crab, live in the sea. They all have two pairs of antennae, compound eyes and many pairs of jointed legs. Crabs have ten legs.

Spiders have eight legs and two parts to their body. All spiders spin silky threads, but only about half of them build webs to catch their prey. Nearly all spiders have poisonous fangs.

Did you know that woodlice are related to crabs? They both have bodies covered in a hard case, or crust, so they are called crustaceans. Woodlice live in damp places to stop their bodies from drying out.

Activity

Make a pooter, to pick up small or fast-moving insects. It works like a small vacuum cleaner. After catching and looking closely at the insects, carefully put them back where you found them. You will need: a small plastic container with a lid, two wide and bendy straws, modelling clay, a small piece of muslin, sticky tape.

1 Take off the lid and make two holes in it. Push the straws through the holes and seal any gaps with modelling clay.

2 Tape a small piece of muslin over the end of one of the straws to stop minibeasts being sucked into your mouth - yuk!

3 Put the lid back on the container.

4 Place the straw without the muslin end near a minibeast and suck hard through the other straw. The minibeast should zoom up the straw into the container.

Animals with Shells

When you find sea shells on the beach, or watch a snail crawling along a path, you are looking at a mollusc. Molluscs have soft bodies that are often protected by strong, hard shells. Most of them live in water and move slowly, although octopuses and squid can suddenly zoom along with a burst of high speed.

▲ An octopus has eight wriggly arms, with strong suckers to hold its meals tightly.

Molluscs

There are three main groups of mollusc. The slug and snail group has a sucker-like foot for walking or swimming. The mussel and clam group has a shell in two parts. The octopus and squid group has a large head with a ring of tentacles. Squid and cuttlefish have a small shell inside their bodies, while octopuses have no shell at all.

▲ Nautiluses are the only member of the octopus and squid group with a shell outside their body. Inside, the shell is divided into about 30 chambers. The animal lives only in the end chamber, which is much larger than the others.

▶ Many sea slugs are brightly coloured, to warn enemies that they are poisonous, or dangerous to touch.

◀ Snails usually have a coiled shell, and can pull their body inside the shell in times of danger.

▶ This female cuttlefish is laying her eggs, closely guarded by the male. Cuttlefish can quickly change colour to startle enemies, blend in with their surroundings or send signals to other cuttlefish.

Look Closer

Molluscs with shells in two parts are called bivalves - 'bi' means two. Special muscles open and close the shell's two parts, which are joined by an elastic hinge. When the shell is open, a 'foot' sticks out so the animal can move and make burrows.

scallop

Bivalves do not have a head. To feed and breathe, they draw water in through a tube called a siphon. They take out food and air from the water, and then pump the waste out of another siphon.

clam

23

Fishes

Fishes are animals that have backbones, live in water and breathe through gills. Most fish are covered in slippery, slimy scales and have a special bag of gas inside their bodies to help them float. Fish have fins instead of arms and legs, and wriggle from side to side to swim along. A fish's body stays at the same temperature as the water around it.

Sharks and rays

Most fishes have a skeleton made of bone, but sharks and rays have a skeleton made of strong, rubbery gristle, called cartilage. These fishes also have rough scales that feel like sandpaper. They are mostly hunters that live in salty water.

▷ Many cichlid fish protect their eggs and young in their mouth or throat, until they are ready to look after themselves.

▲ Many fishes swim in groups called schools or shoals. This helps them to find food and mates, and to watch for danger.

◀ Sharks are a smooth pointed shape to help them swim fast, and they have sharp teeth to bite their prey. As their teeth are broken off or are worn down, new teeth grow to replace them. Some sharks use about 30,000 teeth in a lifetime.

Look Closer

1 A baby salmon hatches out of an egg into a stream or river of freshwater.

2 Sooner or later it swims to the sea and spends several years living and growing there.

3 Eventually, the grown-up salmon makes a special journey back to the stream or river where

it hatched. It recognises the place by the scent of the water.

4 It lays its eggs and then either swims back to the sea or dies. Like most adult fish, salmon do not look after their eggs or young.

Reptiles and Amphibians

The best way to tell the difference between a reptile and an amphibian is to look at their skin. Reptiles, such as snakes and crocodiles, have dry, scaly skin. Amphibians, such as frogs and salamanders, have wet, smooth skin. Both reptiles and amphibians have a bony skeleton, and their bodies are the same temperature as their surroundings. Most of them live in warm places.

Reptiles

There are three main types of reptile: turtles and tortoises, snakes and lizards, and crocodiles and alligators. Most of them live on land. Their tough, waterproof scales stop their bodies drying out. Most reptiles lay eggs with soft, leathery shells.

▶ Most lizards have four legs, sharp claws on their feet and a long tail. They have good eyesight, and can see colours. They like to eat insects. This gecko has millions of tiny hooks on its toes, for gripping and climbing. It can even walk on the ceiling!

◀ Large and dangerous, with a huge snout full of sharp teeth, a crocodile is a fierce hunter. It eats everything, from insects and frogs to fish and birds. Crocodiles are the biggest reptiles alive today.

▶ Their bony shell makes tortoises and turtles look different from other reptiles. Tortoises usually live on land and turtles live in the sea. Sea turtles like this one have flippers so they can swim fast.

▼ A snake uses its forked tongue for tasting and for smelling the air. All snakes eat meat. They kill either using poison or, like this huge boa constrictor, by squeezing their prey to death.

Amphibians

The two main groups of amphibians are frogs and toads, and salamanders and newts. They can live both on the land and in the water. Their skin is not waterproof, so they need to live in damp places to stop their bodies drying out.

▲ The bright colours of this fire salamander mean 'Don't eat me. I'm poisonous!' Salamanders have long bodies and tails. They come out at night, to eat insects, slugs and worms.

Look Closer

1. The female lays lots of eggs in balls of jelly, called frogspawn.

2. 10 days
Tadpoles hatch out of the eggs. They breathe through gills outside their bodies and munch water plants. They wriggle their tails to swim.

3. 7-10 weeks
The tadpoles have grown back legs. They breathe through lungs and eat small insects instead of plants.

4. About 13 weeks
The tadpoles have grown front legs. They look like tiny frogs with tails.

5. About 17 weeks
The tadpoles are now frogs, ready to leave the water and live on land. They are only about as long as an adult's fingernail!

Birds

The smallest bird is only as big as a bee. The largest, the ostrich, is several feet tall. Birds are the only animals that have feathers. A bony skeleton supports their bodies, and they lay eggs with a hard covering called an eggshell. Birds can live all over the world because they keep their body at the same warm temperature all the time.

▷ finger-like flight feathers push and steer the bird through the air

▷ Parrots, such as this scarlet macaw, are strong fliers and tend to fly in flocks. They make loud, screeching calls to keep in touch with each other.

▷ body feathers hug the body, making a smooth shape so the air can slip past easily

◁ scaly legs

Feathers

Did you know that feathers, hair and nails are all made of the same substance? There are three main types of feather. Fluffy down feathers grow close to the skin and help to keep a bird warm. Contour feathers cover a bird's body like a weatherproof jacket and give it a streamlined shape. Flight feathers on the wings and tail help a bird to fly.

▷ Flight feathers can be easily repaired, because the different parts hook together like a zip.

◀ About 40 kinds of birds, such as this penguin, cannot fly. Penguins use their stiff wings to 'fly' under the water instead of in the air. Other flightless birds, such as ostriches and emus, can run very fast.

▲ This male peacock is showing off his colourful feathers to attract a female.

Look Closer

Most birds build nests to keep their eggs and young safe and warm. Female birds usually do most of the work, using twigs, mud, moss, grass, feathers, even spiders' webs.

Male weaver birds knot and twist dried grasses together to make their hanging nest (right).

Eagles nest on top of big, untidy piles of sticks and twigs.

The tailorbird builds its nest inside a pocket of leaves, which it sews together with insect or spider silk, or plant material.

Female eider ducks pull out some of their own feathers to line their nests.

A hummingbird's tiny nest is glued together with sticky spider silk and usually holds only two eggs (right).

Mammals

You are a mammal, and so are bats, cats, elephants and whales. Mammals are the only animals with fur or hair. Baby mammals feed on milk from their mother's body. Most mammals have three kinds of teeth, for cutting, tearing and grinding their food. Like birds, mammals keep their body at the same warm temperature so they can live all over the world, in cold and warm places.

▲ About half of all the different kinds of mammal are rodents. Rodents have four strong gnawing teeth at the front of their mouths. This chipmunk is a rodent, and so are mice, rats, guinea pigs and squirrels.

Baby mammals

Most baby mammals are well developed when they are born. Inside their mother's body, they get food and water through the placenta and cord that link the mother to her baby. A small group of pouched mammals give birth to tiny, poorly developed babies, which grow up inside a pouch. Three unusual mammals - the platypus and two spiny anteaters - lay eggs.

▼ As these saddleback piglets suck their mother's milk, they grow fit and strong. The milk is clean and fresh and the right temperature for them to drink.

A baby kangaroo develops inside its mother's body for about one month. When the baby is born, it is so small it would fit inside a teaspoon! It uses its strong front legs to crawl up to its mother's pouch, where it stays for up to 11 months.

Activity

Can you guess which animals made these tracks?

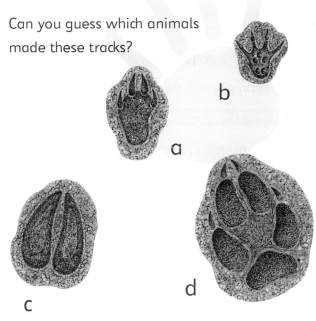

b

a

c

d

a Rabbit b Mouse c Deer d Dog

Big cats, such as tigers, are intelligent, powerful hunters. They have strong claws and teeth, and a rough tongue to scrape meat off bones. Did you know that big cats cannot purr? They can only roar!

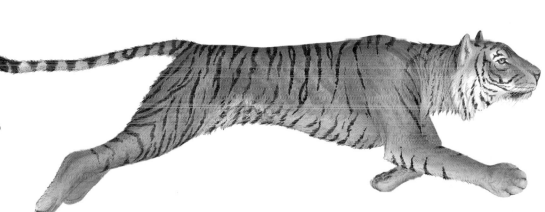

Dolphins, whales and sea cows are the only mammals that spend their whole lives in the sea. They have a smooth body that slides through the water easily. Their strong tail moves up and down to push them along.

Grasslands

Grasslands provide food to many animals around the world. Birds feed upon the seeds and insects living among the grasses. Plant-eating animals, from zebras and gazelles to horses and kangaroos, graze on the grasses. Some plant-eaters, such as hamsters, rabbits and wombats, burrow underground for safety. Meat-eaters such as lions, coyotes and wolves hunt plant-eating animals living nearby.

▲ The giraffe uses its extra long neck to reach leaves and twigs high in the trees. Other animals cannot reach up this high.

Grasslands are full of insects such as locusts, caterpillars and ants. This locust may be part of a visiting swarm of over 1,000 million locusts. Together they eat more grasses and crops than big plant-eaters.

locust

wildebeest

secretary bird

These animals all live in the African grasslands. Zebras eat the tough tops of the grasses, while wildebeests eat the leafy middle bits of the grass plants. Thompson's gazelles nibble the grass after it has been bitten off close to the ground.

Thomson's gazelles live in herds to watch and listen together for danger. They are fast runners, which helps them to escape attacks from speedy cheetahs.

Thomson's gazelle

oxpecker

zebra

Look Closer

Many smaller, furry animals dig burrows underneath grasslands. Here they are safe from enemies and fires, and can keep warm or cool. Some animals store food or sleep in their burrows during the cold winter. Digging burrows mixes up the soil and helps grasses and other plants to grow.

▼ Prairie dogs are not really dogs, but they do bark like dogs to warn each other of danger.

The secretary bird kills snakes with a powerful stamp of its foot. It has long legs to help it walk and run easily through tall grasses.

Oxpeckers climb all over big grazing animals, searching for food such as ticks and flies. Big animals let the oxpeckers do this because the itchy insects bother them.

Forests

Forests are good places for animals to live because there is plenty of shelter and food. Animals live in different parts of the trees and also on the forest floor. The greatest variety of animals lives in rainforests, which are hot and wet all year round. In cooler forests, animals may have to leave during the winter.

Rainforests

Most animals live on the highest level of the steamy rainforest, where there is more sunlight, rain and food. This is called the canopy and is home to chattering monkeys, bats and brightly coloured birds. On the forest floor live bigger, heavier animals, such as pigs and deer, together with striped and spotted hunters such as jaguars and tigers.

Huge harpy eagles swoop down to snatch monkeys and sloths in their sharp talons.

To swing through the trees monkeys have long arms, strong fingers and toes, and long, gripping tails.

Sloths hang upside down from branches, using their long, curved claws as hooks. They sleep for about 18 hours each day.

Scary snakes lurk among the leaves, waiting for a tasty meal to pass by.

The bright blue wings of the male morpho butterflies help them to attract females and may also dazzle enemies.

Tree frogs have sticky toe pads to help them grip slippery and slimy leaves and branches.

The spotted coat of the jaguar helps it to hide as it waits to pounce on its prey.

Deciduous woodlands

Spring is a busy time of year in a deciduous woodland. The bare branches of the trees sprout new leaves, mammals wake up from their winter rest and birds come back to the wood from winter 'holidays' in warmer places. Insects and birds hatch out of eggs and baby mammals are born. The young animals will have plenty of time to grow big and strong before the cold winter weather arrives.

Baby grey squirrels are born in a leafy nest called a drey.

Chiffchaffs and wood warblers make long journeys back to the woods from the warmer lands of North Africa.

Birds such as jays and blue tits pair up, build nests and lay their eggs.

In spring, hedgehogs and dormice wake up from a deep sleep called hibernation.

The woodcock is well camouflaged as she sits on her nest among the fallen leaves of the woodland floor.

Deserts

Deserts often look empty, but a few very special animals live there. Smaller animals hide in burrows during the hot days and come out in the cool nights. Many animals get most of their water from their food and some, such as the kangaroo rat, never drink. Large animals, such as camels and addax, travel long distances to find food and water. Reptiles survive well in deserts because they have waterproof skins and can go without food for a long time.

Sand movers

Hot, soft sand is not easy to travel across. Camels have wide-spreading feet to stop them sinking into the sand. Sidewinder snakes hardly touch the sand's surface, and skinks swim through the sand as if it were water.

▼ Most birds need a daily drink. Male sand grouse use their feathers like a sponge to soak up water, then carry it back to their chicks.

◀ The large ears of the kit fox help it to keep cool by giving off heat like radiators. They also pick up the faint sounds of the small animals the fox hunts for food.

▲ The Bactrian camel lives in Asian deserts, where summers are hot and dry but winters are very cold. Its long fur keeps it warm in winter while its twin humps store fat that contains energy and water.

▶ Sidewinder snakes travel over the sand by leaping sideways. Only part of the snake's body touches the surface at any one time.

◀ The skink's body is a slim, smooth shape for sliding easily through the sand. It wriggles its body from side to side, like a fish in water.

Cold Places

Animals that live in the icy lands around the North or South Pole, or on mountain tops, have to survive fierce winds and freezing cold to stay alive. They may have thick fur or feathers, or fat under the skin to keep them warm. Many animals only visit cold places in the summer to feed or have their young.

▲ The beautiful snow leopard has long, thick fur to keep it warm. Its wide feet work like snowshoes to stop it sinking into the snow.

▼ Never let a polar bear stand on your toes - it weighs as much as six people! These enormous bears kill seals with their huge paws and sharp teeth.

38

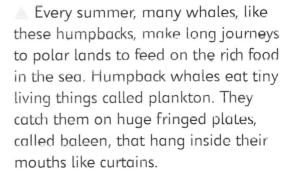
Every summer, many whales, like these humpbacks, make long journeys to polar lands to feed on the rich food in the sea. Humpback whales eat tiny living things called plankton. They catch them on huge fringed plates, called baleen, that hang inside their mouths like curtains.

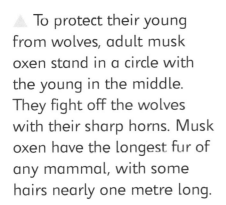
To protect their young from wolves, adult musk oxen stand in a circle with the young in the middle. They fight off the wolves with their sharp horns. Musk oxen have the longest fur of any mammal, with some hairs nearly one metre long.

Look Closer

Every year, the Arctic tern makes the most incredible journey. It flies from the top of the world to the bottom - and back again. This is about 40,000 kilometres!

This small bird nests in the Arctic summer then flies to the Antarctic to feed there during the summer.

Oceans and Shores

Animals live at all levels in the oceans. There are tiny floating animals, jellyfish, fishes and turtles near the surface, whales and squid in the middle levels, and deep-sea fishes, worms and sponges on the ocean floor. Along the shoreline, where the sea meets the land, there is plenty of food for animals such as crabs, worms, fishes and shellfish.

Coral reefs

Coral reefs grow in warm oceans where the water is shallow and clean. They are made from the skeletons of tiny animals called corals, with living coral on top. Many animals live here, from fishes, sea slugs and shellfish, to sea anemones, octopuses and sea snakes.

▲ Food is hard to find in the dark, deep sea. Deep-sea fishes such as this fangtooth, or ogre fish, often have sharp, curved teeth to hold their prey tightly.

▼ Brightly coloured fishes feed and hide among the coral.

Along the shoreline

Shoreline animals are battered by the wind and waves. They have to survive big changes in temperature and moisture levels, as the sea moves up and down the shore with the tides. Yet a huge variety of crabs, worms, shellfish, fish and birds live here because there is plenty of food. A good place to find signs of these creatures is along the strand line - a line of dead seaweed and rubbish thrown up by the tide. Here are some animals to look out for.

Look closely at driftwood for the holes of shipworms and gribbles, which are crustaceans related to woodlice. You may also find stalked goose barnacles on driftwood.

Activity

Make a rock-pool viewer
You will need: an empty yoghurt pot, a craft knife, an elastic band, scissors, thin and clear plastic or clingfilm.

1 Ask an adult to cut out the bottom of the yoghurt pot with the craft knife.

2 Cut out a circle of clear plastic or clingfilm, making it bigger than the bottom of the pot.

3 Stretch the plastic over the base of the yoghurt pot and hold it in place with the elastic band.

4 Dip the plastic-covered end into the rock-pool. Look out for crabs, shrimps, anemones, and small fishes.

Cuttlebone - the shell from inside the body of a common cuttlefish.

Egg cases of rays or dogfishes, called mermaid's purses.

Bones, skeletons or jaws of birds and fish.

Spongy, yellow ball of egg cases of the common whelk (a mollusc with a shell).

Empty crab shells, pushed off by crabs as they moult and grow bigger.

Shells of all shapes and sizes, such as razor shells, cockles and tellins.

Animals in Danger

Can you imagine a world without elephants, pandas and tigers? These are just three of the thousands of animals that are in danger of disappearing from our world. This is because people are hunting them, or changing the places where they live. To help save rare animals we need to protect them from hunting, find out more about how they live, and make sure they have safe places in which to survive in the future.

▼ There are only a few hundred giant pandas left in the world today. They all live in China. Pandas are dying out because the bamboo forests where they live have been cut down. Poachers also kill pandas, although hunting is not allowed any more.

Saving animals

Many rare animals are now protected and live in nature reserves or national parks. Others are looked after in zoos, and may one day be able to go and live in the wild. Laws help to stop parts of rare animals, such as their horns or fur, being sold for a lot of money. You can help to save rare animals by joining a conservation group.

▲ This rare black rhino is being taken to a new home in a national park.

▶ There are only about 9,000 blue whales left in the world. Thousands were killed for their oil and meat. Hunting is now banned, but they are still in danger.

▶ Tigers have very few wild places left in which to live. People also kill them for their beautiful fur coats and other body parts. Fewer than 5,000 tigers are left in the wild.

◀ There are only about 400 mountain gorillas left today. Most of the forests where they live have been destroyed, and they are hunted for food. They also die from human diseases.

Extinct animals

When every one of a particular kind of animal has died and there are no more left, that animal is extinct. All these animals are extinct, gone forever.

These animals died out because of things people did to them. Some were killed by hunters. People took away the homes or food supplies of others.

moa

quagga

dodo   tasmanian wolf

Animal Detective Quiz

Now you can be an animal detective, and track down the answers to this fun quiz. The animals are all in this book somewhere! Look for clues in the questions: what sort of animal is it about, what are they doing, where do they live? You can use the Contents list and the Index to help you find the right page. Good luck!

Can you find. . .?

1 five animals that lay eggs?
2 three poisonous animals?
3 five rare animals?
4 three animals with wings?

Which. . .?

1 Which bird can kill snakes?
2 Which bird has a bill like a sieve?
3 Which animal likes to eat ants?
4 Which animal can run as fast as a car?

Why. . .?

1 Why does a bushbaby have big eyes?
2 Why does a curlew have such a long beak?

3 Why do tree frogs have sticky toes?
4 Why does a kangaroo have a pouch?
5 Why does a giraffe have a long neck?
6 Why does a male peacock have colourful feathers?

How. . .?

1 How do snakes smell things?
2 How fast can a sailfish swim?
3 How long do termites take to build their tower?

4 How many legs does a millipede have?
5 How many teeth may a shark use in its lifetime?
6 How many legs does an octopus have?

Answers on page 48

Index

A

alligators 26
amphibians 7, 26-27
animal detective quiz 44-45
anteaters 13, 30
antennae 20, 21
ants 18, 32
arthropods 6

B

babies 7, 16-17, 25, 27,
  30, 36
bats 9, 30, 34
bears 12, 38
bees 6, 20
beetles 20
bills 13
birds 7, 9, 13, 17, 28-29,
  32-33, 34-35, 36, 39
bivalves 23
bones 7
brains 7
burrows 32, 33, 36
bushbabies 10, 45
butterflies 16, 17, 20, 34

C

camels 36-37
camouflage 15, 23, 35
caterpillars 12, 17, 32
cats 30, 31
centipedes 20
cheetahs 8
chimpanzees 19
chipmunks 30
clams 23
claws 14, 15, 31
climbing 9, 26
communication 10
coral reefs 15, 40
cows 12
coyotes 32
crabs 6, 21, 30, 40-41
crawling 8

crocodiles 7, 12, 26
crustaceans 21, 41
curlews 13, 45
cuttlefish 22-23, 41

D

deer 34
deserts 36-37
dogs 12, 16
dolphins 7, 31

E

eagles 6, 13, 34
ears 7, 10
eggs 16-17, 18, 25, 27,
  28-29, 30, 35, 41
elephants 7, 12, 16, 30, 42
extinct animals 42-43
eyes 7, 10-11

F

fangs 14, 21
feathers 7, 28-29, 36
fins 7, 24
fish 7, 9, 14, 15, 19, 24-25,
  40-41
flamingos 13
flies 13
flying 7, 8, 9, 28
flying fish 9
food 7, 12-13
forests and woods 34-35
foxes 12, 37
frogs 7, 16, 26-27, 34, 45
fur and hair 7, 28, 30

G

gazelles 32-33
geckos 26

gills 7, 24, 27
giraffes 32, 45
gliding 8, 9
goats 9
gorillas 7, 43
grasslands 32-33
guinea pigs 30

H

hamsters 32
hearing 7, 10
hedgehogs 7, 35
hibernation 35
horses 12, 16, 32
humans 7
hunting 12, 14-15, 31

I

insects 6, 7, 9, 18, 20-21,
  32-33
invertebrates 6

J

jaguars 7, 34
jellyfish 6, 20, 40

K

kangaroos 31, 32, 45
koalas 12

L

legs 6, 7, 8, 20
lemurs 11
leopards 38
lions 32
lizards 7, 26
lobsters 20, 21
locusts 32

M

mammals 6, 7, 30-31
mandrills 6
metamorphosis 17
mice 30, 35
migration 35, 39
milk 7, 30
millipedes 6, 20, 45
minibeasts 20-21
moles 11
molluscs 6, 22-23, 41
monkeys 6, 9, 34
mosquitoes 13
movement 6, 7, 8-9
musk oxen 39

N

nautiluses 22
nests 29, 35
newts 7, 27
night time animals 10
noses 10-11

O

octopuses 6, 14, 22, 40, 45
opossums 9
ospreys 14
ostriches 28, 29
owls 17
oxpeckers 33
oysters 6

P

pandas 42
parrots 28
peacocks 29, 45
penguins 29
pigs 30, 34
plankton 39
platypuses 30
poisonous animals 14, 21, 23, 27

Polar regions 38-39
pooters 21
porcupines 15
prairie dogs 33
pupas 17

R

rabbits 32
rats 30, 36
rays 24
reptiles 7, 26-27, 36
rhinos 43
rodents 30
running 8

S

salamanders 26 27
scales 24
scallops 23
scorpions 17
sea anemones 6, 15, 40, 41
sea cows 31
sea urchins 6
senses 6, 7, 10-11
sharks 15, 24-25, 45
shells 6, 22-23, 27, 40-41
shrimps 21, 41
sight 7, 10-11
skeletons 7, 24, 26, 28, 41
skinks 36-37
skunks 15
sloths 34
slugs 8, 22-23, 40
smell 10-11, 14
snails 6, 8, 20, 22-23
snakes 7, 11, 12, 15, 26-27, 34, 36-37, 40, 45
social behaviour 18-19, 28
spiders 6, 13, 14, 20, 21
sponges 6, 40
squid 22, 40
squirrels 7, 30, 35
swimming 8, 9, 27, 29

T

tadpoles 27
tails 9, 34
talons 14
taste 10-11
teeth 12, 13, 14, 25, 26, 30, 31, 40
tentacles 22
termites 18, 45
tigers 31, 34, 42-43
toads 7, 27
tongues 11, 13, 31
tortoises 7, 26-27
touch 10-11
turtles 26-27, 40

V

vertebrates 6, 7

W

walking 8
wasps 6, 10, 18
waxwings 7
whales 30, 31, 39, 40, 43
wildebeest 32
wings 7, 9, 20, 28
wolves 12, 32, 39
wombats 32
woodlice 21
worms 6, 20, 40-41

Z

zebras 32-33

Acknowledgements

Photographs

Page 9tl Stephen Dalton/NHPA; p10tr G I Bernard/NHPA; p10br Stephen Dalton/NHPA; p12b William Ervin/SPL; p14tr Dietmar Nill/BBC Wildlife; p15tr Hellio & Van Ingen/NHPA; p16b Christophe Ratier/NHPA; p17cl John Cancalosi/NHPA; p19t E A Janes/NHPA; p21tr Jürgen Freund/BBC Wildlife; p22c Frank Greenaway/Natural History Museum; p23c Georgette Douwma/BBC Wildlife; p24br Max Gibbs/Oxford Scientific Films; p26bl A N T/NHPA p28r Stephen Dalton/NHPA; p29tr Tony Craddock/SPL; p30bl David Woodfall/NHPA; p31br Doc White/Planet Earth Pictures; p33br John Cancalosi/BBC Wildlife; p36tr Stephen Krasemann/NHPA; p38tr Alan & Sandy Carey/Oxford Scientific Films p38b Thomas D Magelsen/BBC Wildlife; p39tr Rick Rosenthal/BBC Wildlife; p40tr Gregory Ochocki/SPL; p40background & b B Jones & M Shimlock/NHPA; p42 Jany Sauranet/SPL; p43 Jen & Des Bartlett/Oxford Scientific Films; front cover Art Wolfe/Tony Stone Images

The illustrations are by:

Sophie Allington 7cr,
Norman Arlott 13br, 45tl,
Julian Baker 9c,
John Butler 17b, 37b, 39c, 45c,
Marina Durante 4, 8t, 13t, 17t, 19c, 21br, 31tr, 41t, 45br
Brin Edwards 15b,
Michael Gaffney 29cl, 39br,
Mick Loates 7c, 9bl, 15cr,
Simon Mendez 5, 12, 18b, 18cr, 34, 35, 41b, 45bl,
Sean Milne 9br, 11tl, 13bl, 23b, 23t, 25b, 29b, 33, 44bl,
Damian Quayle 11tr, 21bl, 31tl, 44tr,
Paul Richardson 6r, 7cb, 8b, 9cr, 31cr, 37tr, back cover tr
S. Roberts 6c, 6b, 7l, 7ct, 7t, 7br, 11b, 13c, 15cl, 22tr, 27t, 27bl, 30, 43, 44cr,
Treve Tamblin 14, 19b, 25c, 44br, 45tr, back cover bl
P. Visscher 6bl,
David Wood 3, 27cr,

Key t = top b = bottom c = centre r = right l = left

Quiz answers

Can you find?

1. owl, butterfly, termite, salmon, frog
2. blue-ringed octopus, sea slug, fire salamander
3. giant panda, black rhino, tiger, blue whale, mountain gorilla
4. birds (osprey, owl, parrot, penguin, Arctic tern), butterfly, flying fish

Which?

1. secretary bird
2. flamingo
3. giant anteater
4. cheetah

Why?

1. to help it see in the dark
2. to find juicy worms hidden deep in the mud
3. to help them grip slippery and slimy leaves and branches
4. to protect its baby while it develops
5. to reach leaves and twigs high in the trees
6. to attract a female

How?

1. with their tongue
2. up to 100 kilometres per hour
3. up to 50 years
4. up to 350 legs
5. some sharks use about 30,000 teeth in a lifetime
6. eight legs